Gen

for the Edwardses

Gen

Jonathan Edwards

Seren is the book imprint of
Poetry Wales Press Ltd.
57 Nolton Street, Bridgend, Wales, CF31 3AE
www.serenbooks.com
facebook.com/SerenBooks
twitter@SerenBooks

The right of Jonathan Edwards to be identified as
the author of this work has been asserted in accordance
with the Copyright, Designs and Patents Act, 1988.

ISBN: 978-1-78172-473-6
ebook: 978-1-78172-474-3
Kindle: 978-1-78172-475-0

A CIP record for this title is available from the British Library.

The publisher acknowledges the financial assistance of the Welsh Books Council.

Cover artwork: 'Hard to Get', 2011, Oil on Linen by Kevin Sinnott.

Author photograph: Aubrey Edwards.

Printed in Bembo by Bell & Bain Ltd, Glasgow.

Contents

1

2

3

4

1

Sing Song Spring Song

Begin again. The birds are up to what
they're up to always, aren't they, listen, those
persistent little fuckers, and the sun
is shining down on courting couples, like
a high-watt bulb, say, in a top-floor flat,
might shine its little heart out on a room
of high-grade hashish plants, and your breath loyally
or out of habit, say, goes out, goes in.
So what *now* is is as good a time as any
to get up off your arse boy and begin.

Begin again. The love that won't be yours
is somewhere else for good while here, this hair
makes the wind real; these heads look bob like blonde
lifebuoys. In a café window there,
girls jiggle straws look in their early-season
iced cappuccinos, look out at the hairy
passing men and speak like highly-sexed
football commentators. Milky blossom
or birdshit falls. Church bells or smartphones ring.
So brush off your best threads now, boy. Begin.

Begin again, as men in hi-vis vests
who work all day in weather roast the colour
of rose tattoos that bloom there on their shoulders,
or turn a corner to a sudden breeze
and hug themselves. These mirrored imitation
Ray-Bans capture pictures of the high street
in spitting rain, shops fill with everything
that could be yours, a gull opens its beak
as if to sing, but dips look for a chip.
So wipe dust from your lips now, boy. Begin

again, now, as washing on a line
impersonates a ship look in full sail,
and Mrs Wilson, in her landlocked garden,
says goodbye to the harbour with a wave.
The trees will soon be fat with leaves like green
candyfloss, and daffodils in yellow
post-op canine collars turn the faces
they don't have towards the sun, or have
their stems, their hearts, look, broken by the wind.
Pick up your bloody pen now, boy. Begin.

Gen

So here they come, around the corner,
bouncing, flouncing, boho
beehives, tattooed, corduroy-looned, sneakered
scumbags, skinheads, brogue-shod uni fools, or
look, they're me, they're you, but slightly
cooler, lust- and roll-up-fuelled, artfully
spectacled idea junkies, pushing,
selling, any one of us could be
John Lennon, Jesus, coke and sneezes
forced through nostrils that are pinned
or pierced. Look, these feather-boa'd
vegans or these leopardskinned
animals, with their X-rated
bodies, their needs never sated
by hands-free friends or look, their palm-held
search engines, their razor'd heads turned
by beauty or a global crisis, these masters
of their own devices. For every word
they've #'d or abbreviated, each god
they've never worshipped, every song
they've downloaded, shook their arses to or sung,
I say bow down, bow down, the young, the young.

Kurt Cobain Proposes to Courtney Love, TJs, Newport, December 1991

Some young dude staggering from the station,
all jeans and grimace, all tufty coat
and peep-toe sneakers – that's nothing
new around these parts. He rubs
his eyes, approaches this first stranger:
*Excuse me, do you know the way to a place
called TJs?* That voice
he has. A mile away, Courtney

Love is sound checking, warming up. Rain
comes down as he passes the ruined
castle, crosses the bridge
statistics say more than thirty people
will jump from that year. *Nevermind*
has been Billboard #1
for six weeks now. What
exactly does a human being do

with that much love? I am four
miles away and twelve years old, and Kurt Cobain
is walking through Newport, three years
too early for me. At the door
of TJs, his nose-ringed
biggest fan in the world
just tells him the price, stamps
his hand. Inside,

his eyes accustom and he spots
her, at the bar, back to the room. Her
mane. Her little girl's
dress. People are brought into being by moments
like this: Kurt Cobain is crossing
the room in TJs, Newport, is falling
to his knees. The cold
floor through ripped jeans. The barman leaps

across the counter to deal
with some punter, and the bouncer,
grinning, gets in the way
as one girl punches another. Of course,
there are those who say all this is folklore,
legend, gossiped up by someone
with a romantic imagination
or a marketing background. I am twelve years old

and dreaming in a room lined with posters
of footballers and, on Newport Bridge,
a couple are walking hand-in-hand,
the man pausing now, perhaps, to light
a cigarette. In that sudden spark,
someone passing might almost glimpse his face,
before he turns away,
before he walks again into the dark.

Olympic 100m Final, Seoul, 1988

In the middle of his adolescence, my brother gets up
and turns on the TV. A line of men like none I've seen:
the blocks make them quadrupeds; their eyeballs eyeball us. *SET!* –

their arses rise in unison. One day this moment, now, will be
retro. The starter fires his gun at history and they're off, down a track
that's our street for the rest of August. What we're too young to know

is the winner's immigrant childhood, his single mother's three jobs,
how he hid in the school toilets from bullies. What he'll never know
is how, although we'll fight each other over who gets to be

Carl Lewis in our games that summer, it won't quite beat the way
we danced when that man crossed the line, pissed over the world record,
how we sang his name. Ben Johnson. How we loved him, for a day.

Harry Houdini on Newport Bridge, May 1905

He stands a hundred feet above a river
that's popular with suicides and lovers.
He stands there in the limelight and the weather
in padlocks, chains, a straitjacket and his immaculate
moustache: the whole town, gathered, watching, breathes
in. He stands a hundred feet above the river and

leaps. Meanwhile, in the crowd, my grandfather is busy
being fifteen; he's presently engaged
in tying the shoelaces of a policeman
to those of a vicar, lifting
handkerchieves from pockets
to swap them with each other. Harry Houdini

has been what, a minute underwater
and, in the crowd, hands are being raised
to mouths. A day off for my grandfather
from the family village butcher's:
he looks up at the chains
on the watches of his father, his grandfather. A minute

and a half: a woman on the bank
points towards a darkness in the river,
slowly turning to a bobbing head, moustache,
a waving hand, a cheer. The woman starts
to cry: her husband reaches for his handkerchief.
A policeman pulls a vicar from his feet.

My Mother Cuts Her Arm, 1955

She's eight years old and there in her front garden,
waiting for the moment when her father
comes home from work or strolls around the corner,
fills the terraced street up with himself,
swinging in his hand his bag, his lunchbox,
the chocolate roll he always brings home for her.

She's eight years old and there in her front garden.
The railing-tops are shaped like leaves and golden
and sharp and pointed – look at them – and waiting.
She hears him whistle now before she sees him
and in the rush to rise she trips, slips, falls
on the railings look which catch her – there –

underneath her arm. What she remembers
is something warm and wrong she says, right here,
the red that spoiled her father's white work shirt.
Her skin flapped open like a broken door.
They told her she just missed an artery.

The next day she was reading *Treasure Island*,
with a week off school, a fussing mother
and a lifetime supply of chocolate rolls.
That evening, she heard tinkle after tinkle
there beneath her window and looked out

to see her father, his white sleeves rolled up,
a hacksaw in his hand, sandpaper ready,
and that sharp leaf from every single railing
on the ground. A harvest of guilt and metal.

Sixty years, and standing in her kitchen,
she looks down now out of that bedroom window
to see her father. Now he straightens up
to speak to Mrs Morris from next door,
gesticulating with his shining hacksaw.
Now the setting sun, that mid-May moment,
catches his glasses, makes him brilliant.

My Father Buying Sweets, 1956

So here he is, eleven, a little bugger,
with his neat curls, his comprehensive training
to be my lookalike. His mother's voice
chases him down the terrace, as he swaggers to the music
of the coins in his pocket: his school tie, flipped
over his shoulder, is a silk scarf sported by an artist,
strutting from one absinthe-joint to another
in 19th-century Paris. Now he looks in the window
of Mrs Bullen's sweet shop:
the reflection puts his face in a jar
of chocolate toffees, grinning. Chimes
announce him as he steps inside, the shop
Mrs Bullen's front room. Fearsome
in pastels, she emerges, eyes him, places weights
on one side of the scales, sweets
on the other, offers him
all she has of justice. A clatter
into the till and he's out
and walking home, a paper bag
full in his palm. There are years
in which the shop will go to bedsits, the bedsits
to ruin, my father's mouth will bloom
with fillings, but now his evening stretches
deliciously ahead, and he pauses helpfully
beneath a streetlight, so we can watch him
lift one gleaming thing from the bag, unwrap it,
raise it to his lips –
so I can taste all the butter, cream, the sugar,
here, on the tip of my tongue.

My Father Crashes a Car, 1965

So there he is look, there behind the wheel
of a company car, in waiting-to-be-retro
suit he'll one day wear in photographs
I'll see, there with the curly hair he'll later
give to me I'm not around to take it
yet. He pulls away: what's in his head's

the girl with all the hair and polka dots
he saw outside the 'Stute last Friday night.
Here's Newport then, in February: the sky
is working through its endless repertoire
of greys and, as he heads towards Stow Hill,
the one thing he would not expect to see's

what's there: a girl in a canary yellow
bathing suit stretched on an E-type bonnet.
She's there to market something; what she does is
send his head now spinning on his neck,
like for this moment it's the very world
spinning on its axis. Who could really

think a young man under such conditions
would see the slowing, green and yes, expensive
car he's sailing merrily towards
now all he sees is yellow? He gets out
to check the damage, his pre-air bag head
and there's a moment now, before the girl

in yellow turns towards him and just laughs,
before the man in the green car has punched him
to the floor and everything's gone black –
there is this moment he's still not forgot,
when the man's wife leaps from the passenger seat
and through the smoke, my father sees an angel

sprint towards him, wearing polka dots.

My Uncle Smoking a Pipe, 1986

So there he is, all through my childhood, sitting
on the sofa, going nowhere, making
you know, roughly as much smoke as any

steam train. Here among the skirting boards,
the candlesticks, the weather for the region
is fog and there among the clouds he's playing

peek-a-boo. Between these Anaglypta'd
walls, the smut, the smog of London town
is gathered: squint a bit and Big Ben's peeping

through. All through my childhood, Christmases,
my father's birthdays, there, my uncle rolling
tobacco in the rhythm of his thinking,

plucking from the air my father's jokes,
rubbing them between his thumb and finger,
then offering this punch line: one enormous

lungful of that smoke. It thickens now,
it darkens: see my cousins and my aunt
find each other just by voice, by touch,

and the location of the dining table,
the door's a mystery. All through my childhood,
my gran announcing ailments, births and deaths,

my unrepentant, puffing uncle filling
and filling up the world with his own breath.

Teenage Son

Hair like someone scribbled out his face
and a look like he did, you might find him
on the top deck, on a half fare into town,
or trying for a pint in The Fox and Hounds
in my voice. He has an old man's shoulders
and my wife's eyes. I call him Mr Cold Ears,
with those huge bloody headphones always plugged in.
He's what I love, but never fell in love with.

This morning, I breakfasted with my stunt double.
In the middle of the night, I poke my head
around his door: he's on some computer game,
tells me he's just killed Saddam Hussein.
His chin is fluffy as a chrysalis.
Photos of body parts stick out from under his bed.

Days of 1995

Here she comes, flouncing down the corridor,
wearing her rolled-up skirt, her reputation,
a Stacey or a Hayley on each arm,
catwalking from DT to double German.
Her high heels echo down the corridor,
they echo off these ceilings and these walls,
the way the sound of Steve McQueen's baseball
must have echoed round his cooler cell
in *The Great Escape*. For they are shoes
with letters written about them, which schedule meetings
between her mother and the grim Headteacher,
between the Head and some grinning boy's father.
She flicks her head, because of how it makes
her hair go, laughs her laugh – the one that makes
her tongue show. You saw her once outside The Castle
with some bloke old enough to be her father,
and Jonno says she hopped in a Cortina
one night on the back road out of Risca.
A few weeks and you're out of here this summer.
Faint heart, if you were going to say something,
it would need to be now – now as she's passing
or strutting, from DT into her future.
And look, in her shirt pocket, there's a packet
of Marlboro between you and her heartbeat.

House Party at Tanya's, 1995

The word was passed in Maths, in double Physics,
by boys on street corners, football pitches,
behind a teacher's back, between the clack-
on-clack of balls around the pool halls. Come

Friday night, nice-jeaned, we walked the streets
in nervous gangs, jabbed cigarettes towards
the night, in the universal sign language for
Look at me, I'm great. Our jackets bulged

with all we could get from the corner shop,
with our sleight-of-hand, our sweet talk,
our cultivated bumfluff and our brothers'
NUS cards. At home, our fathers

opened doors on empty cupboards. We turned
a corner, found a terraced house with music
pouring from the chimney, ran our hands
through our hair, dipped inside and there

was chaos, carnage, every pot plant
an ashtray, every ashtray a sick bag,
the carpet a dancefloor and the dancefloor
sticky. Listen, this girl here

was leading some boy upstairs by the hand,
this boy launching himself a little like
a basketball towards this group of girls
to see where he might land, to look round at

anything was to see bottles, glasses,
cans, and through a doorway there a glimpse,
a glance, a boy there, on his tongue a disc
he's swallowing. The music tried

to make up by its volume what it lacked
in everything. Reader, if you take my hand
and step outside with me now, before good sense
or homeowners return, before the loss

of consciousness, virginity,
the bus fare home, my two front teeth,
there is one moment, on this terraced street,
we can get back to, if we both try hard:

there is a moment, here, among
the broken streetlights, krooklok'd cars,
this swirling wind, this being young,
and there, a massive, endless sky of stars.

Days of 2005

See that boy there look, lying in the street?
A tattered hoodie next to bare
skin, now waking slowly, sleepyheading
on the kerb. He stumbles slightly

as he gets to his feet. There is a ringing
in his ears and something in his mouth
isn't right. He checks his pockets:
no phone, no cash, but there, somehow,

his debit card. He runs his fingers
along the numbers. There is a whisky
bottle round here somewhere
and he's shivering, as something starts to move him

through what he sees are terraced streets,
curtains tight-closed with lives behind,
each roof cherry-topped
by a satellite dish. His shadow is big

beneath a streetlight as he checks his watch to see
the hopeless hours till work. He wants a taxi
to a hotel, train station, pub
that's open but, as he comes round the corner,

he realises he's been down this street before.
He's ready to give up
completely when he sees the pale,
pale light of a phone box up ahead,

and is just reaching for the receiver
when he thinks once, twice, of phoning home.
Dawn is beginning to make real
the place this is, put colour in the cheeks

of car after car, pick out detail —
has that one got the keys left in?
Now a phone is ringing, somewhere, in a room
and someone better answer it —

someone better answer it, and soon.

Runt

I got home to find *POLICE LINE DO NOT CROSS* taped across the door. Inside, my mother was sitting with her head in her hands, while a little man who smelt of Johnnie Walker tried to look up her skirt.

'Detective,' I said, 'what's going on?'

'We've arrested your father on suspicion of being a perfectly sound bloke who's never caused a ha'p'orth of trouble to anyone in his life. It's a serious charge. He's looking at a twenty-five-year stretch.'

Around us, policemen were dusting down evidence for prints and bagging it: the strawberry cupcakes my father had brought home for us that morning, his collection of birthday cards, still on display on the mantelpiece, even the flowers in the hanging baskets he tended all summer. In the garden, I found them taking a statement from Big Jim, who said he drank three and a half pints of Best with my old man every Friday, and my father always insisted on buying the first round.

We spent the night on the hard, luminous chairs at the police station. It was some time after dawn when they arrested my mother on suspicion of being a hard-working, salt-of-the-earth character, who'd sooner starve herself than see anyone else go without cake.

'Alright Detective,' I said, 'that's enough. I'll come quietly.'

'Oh no,' he said, as the walkie-talkie in his hand burst into life. 'Oh no, we won't be needing you. You're perfectly free to go.'

2

Writers in the Movies

pound their typewriters and wipe their brows,
whisky bottles open on their desks. They're in
Havana, Madrid, the past, the middle

of a revolution or a civil war. They're Hemingway
or Johnny Depp, DiCaprio or Hunter S
in his youth. To write well, it's necessary

to work all night, pausing only
to make furious love
to Keira Knightley, preferably against

a wall, as bombs fall in the streets outside
and all their struggles whistle through their brains.
A quick cigarette, a superficial

conversation about their fathers,
then back to work for hours or a few frames,
till the sun rises on their neatly-piled

manuscripts, their dishevelled, just-brushed hair,
and they go to the window with coffee,
stroking their chests. Before the day begins,

and they turn to save the world or wake a lover,
there is that moment, that one moment, when
all the writers in the movies stare

at the air. The empty air. The empty air.

Samuel Taylor Coleridge Walking from The Queen's Head, Gray's Inn, to Hornsby's and Co., Cornhill, to Buy an Irish Lottery Ticket, November 1793

At twenty-one, he needs something big to happen
to cover his bar tab, run up trying to escape
thought of his debts. What his life is going like

is this: the blown scholarship
nothing that can't be dealt with
by opium; ladies with abracadabra

clothes to make the girl who will not love
disappear. A night
of weighing up options: on one hand,

the army, in the other,
a pistol. Then drunken inspiration, a solution
to his life and here he is, on his way,

inventing a new walk –
the wobble-stride. He's walking, walking,
writing in his head To Fortune, a poem

to read whose rhyming couplets
is to hear him walking
now. A month or two and his brother

will clear his debts,
a day or so and his lottery ticket
will lie in a ditch, a couple of weeks

and To Fortune will appear in The Morning Chronicle,
his first published poem, and they'll pay a guinea,
which he'll try – and find it good –

against his teeth.

Servant Minding a Seat for his Master Before a Performance of *The Rivals*, Covent Garden Theatre, 1775

I do what I'm told, me. What does sir need?
Some pleb to take a load off, guard your seat,
to sit right back and put his paid-for feet

up, three hours, four, sat on your hands –
guv'nor, I'm your man. Sir, master, boss,
it might seem wasted time but it's no loss –

my master is a god to me. The one
thing that bothers me is Gossip John,
who minds the next seat over, passes hours,

now whispering about our master's trips
after dark to some house on the docks,
now of our lady's preference for cloth

to silk, or how she passes like the breeze
through servants' rooms which echo with her squeals.
It's all a gas for John to sell or share

their weaknesses, their joys. I wouldn't dare:
he spills the beans and turns to me and winks;
I blush and turn away and bow my head

and say the thing that's often been heard said
about my master by the Duke of Gloucester –
his dignity, his wit. It's a relief

when master comes, leading his frilly daughter.
Now nobody would see, we're up so quick,
the subtle look that flicks from her to me,

as master's arse slips snug onto the seat
I've warmed for him. I've never seen a play,
but as I walk away from *this* performance,

the sound of clapping, listen, dogs my heels.

Welsh Flag on the Wall
of Richard Burton's Dressing Room,
Broadway, 1983

I've seen the lot: the nights he's come back late,
the janitor calling *Okay, Mr Burton?*,
his coat heavy with Scotch and sunk a drop
or two or hurled a bottle at this wall

I hang on. Me, I can't see how that room-long
mirror helps: he sits there making faces
at himself. I float above him. He
should take a tip from me and stand or stand

for something. Sometimes he speaks to me – oh, mostly
morbid stuff. Sometimes, far gone, he'll call me
Elizabeth. And who are all these others –
Cleo, Sal, Cordelia, the miner's

son, born Richard Jenkins – in his head?
He looks in his own eyes and says the words
of someone else. I've seen the frowns, the smiles
and all the rest and do my best for him:

as he steps through the door, I flutter faintly
in the air conditioning, raise a paw,
but nothing helps. His born pretender's breath
goes on, wheezing *Myself, myself, myself.*

Food Tester

I'd give my life for his. This poisoned fruit
that could cut short his breath or break his heart,
this leg of pork that makes him sick for days
or weeks slips easily across my lips

and down my throat. You get a feel for this,
a nose, and do the work by weight, by touch,
to cut the chance, the risk. The merest hint
of something strong in a pitcher of milk,

or in this tender flesh a tint, a fleck,
to make a bite of it – just one – a bite
of death. I work alone and with my friends:
the apparatus of pipettes and scales,

the grim art of this business and the science
of my instinct. Does one drop in water
bubble or change colour, does a bit
dabbed on the wrist, just here, affect the skin,

cause it to itch, to rise and, more than this,
can chef this morning look you in the eye?
What do you know about his wife, his mother,
the sous chef's background or the politics

of the waiter? I would give my life for his.
I've never seen him but I've heard he eats
like a pig: a mouthful of mutton, chased
with a fistful of capon, spitting words

and food across the table. Today, I face
this bird, this side of beef, this bread, this meat
and this forkful, right here. The one I'm raising
to my lips now as I feel them burn.

The Pianist at The Grand

What are you but a head behind a desk?
Can't you do something, mister? You just sit there,
your foot busy on the accelerator,
but your long bonnet going slowly nowhere.
The hero of my poem's doing nothing,

nada. Your music is another matter.
At the end of your hands, a troop of gymnasts,
who want to twist and twirl, who want to whirl
and dance, to do some mischief in this world.
And look, my bobbing head just can't say *No*

to your left hand, while your right fingers solo,
get busy, crazy, get excited, go
apeshit, take it further, faster, masters
of their own devices, slow at last
and sway, carried away on your behalf.

Meanwhile, your face is waiting for a bus.
The furthest you might go's a single glance
towards the door, at some hotshot who's just
strolling in, a quick nod to the singer.
I wonder whether they're really your fingers,

which scurry, whir, near and far, which are
a party or a blur. Yet when you're done
and chatting with a guest or a musician,
I watch that same calm face, and your right hand
that's drumming on the bar, that's rattling change.

Crocodile

All afternoon, your body plays it cool
in the deep end, sends your head up for a peek,
a periscope with teeth. A rock-shaped head

among head-shaped rocks, your variegated tints
are dangerous as a man in camouflage paint.
You stepped from prehistory into this century

on plaything legs. Your females lay around
a hundred eggs. Now you drag your monstrous tail
and reputation onto a rock to sunbathe.

Your brothers are a game of snap, your boredom
a rabbit-trap, your happiness a drawer
of knives. You slip again beneath the surface

for fish, for meat. What can we do with our lives,
you say, but follow our smiles? Or our teeth.

Giraffe

So there you are. Your record-breaking neck's
your thing, your USP, your raison d'être,
your marketing department and your fame,
the reason now for me to ask just who

put that little head up on that crane?
You know the loneliness of being strange,
the happiness of being you. You roam,
you amble and you range, and your neck goes

and goes and there's the stilt walk of your face,
the thrill ride of your throat, your bumbly grace,
your gangly bliss. That neck, that massive *this*,
is blank cheque, cash cow, revenue, the source

of all those gift shop fluffy toys of you.
You who stole the hooves right off a horse
when it looked away now swagger, sway
out of another world, a madman's dream,

and here you are: your lovebit/fleabit neck
reaches for high leaves, and when you get
up you climb the staircase of yourself
into an attic lit by stars. You are

a viewing tower look, a periscope,
an early draft, your shape a jest, a joke
that walks, but when I look into your eyes
which move, which glint, which *think*, in all that dark,

which seem to speak, or seem to want to try,
it's then I see what all this is about:
the *you* beneath the surface, trapped inside,
the *me* that's in you, trying to get out.

Lions Asleep

So look, don't bother us, we're only sleeping,
our arms around each other and our eyes
tight closed. We drift, we doze: here on the hearthside
rugs our manes are, holding the hot-water
bottles of each other, we are dreaming.

Do not disturb. Don't make us toss or turn,
we're having forty winks, our bodies coiled
or curled around each other, so it's never
clear where I end, where he begins.
This glass is thin. Don't bang, don't knock. We're in

the land of nod so turn that flash right off
and tell your young, face-painted for the day
with our markings, roaring to be us,
not to butt this window with their heads
now please. Asleep in bed is where we are.

We know the zoo map makes us cover stars,
but jog on, please, go see the seals, who'll show
it all for sprats like strip-club dollars thrown
in their direction. Leave us here, beneath
the covers of each other. As a treat,

if you are very good, we'll make your day
a little later, get up, pace about
a bit, or raise our heads, offer our pink
yawns, but don't be fooled. Beneath these snores,
we think our thoughts. And death sleeps in these paws.

Autumn Song

I walked through a late autumn world –
world was a place of leaves –
all circled look, all swirled –
and bumbling, tumbling,
bouncing, flouncing,
making the wind real,
or if they spun look there like thoughts,
then what's this one
I reached, I caught
between my finger and my thumb –
oh how they rise, how ride –
is this a piece of autumn's fuddled mind?

I walked down a late autumn street –
street was a world of crunch
and unleaf-coloured leaves,
all rustling, wrestling,
rusting, resting,
deep-fried to the touch.
These trees sit in the barber's chair –
these blondes, these reds, these browns –
these cuttings falling to the ground,
this salon in the open air,
as listen, now the rain comes down,
does its shampoo and set –
wind runs a hand through mountainside's brunette.

I walked through a late autumn life –
leaves falling through the world –
these parachutists look, these suicides –
beneath the wheels
of cars which speed,
the heels of well-heeled girls,
leaves everywhere,
now in my hair,
now getting up my nose,
now sticking themselves to the road –
this superglue, this rain –
now putting themselves in the post
with no address or name,
but everything they have of hope
of getting home, of getting home again.

I walked through autumn's muddled head
and all its thoughts were leaves,
celebrating their own deaths,
going shades of gold which said,
Take a look at me.
Trees turn themselves to skeletons,
do shadow puppets in the sun,
and make a bride of everyone
on our late autumn street,
by throwing their confetti at our feet.

Song of the Retail Park Tree

All day, the sun umbrellas outside Caffè Nero
mimic me. I am bought
en masse from a gardening supply store
in the Midlands and will be paid for
in 36 easy instalments. My watering schedule
is outlined in the staff handbook. My roots
do not go deep. Somewhere, in an office in the city,
there is a version of me
in blueprint. Here, a gull harvests
french fries from a McDonalds carton
on the pavement in front of me
and cries. Nobody will ever carve a heart
into my trunk, my bark. No one will ever
pick fruit from me, in this, in any, weather.

All day, the awning outside Subway flutters
its eyelashes at me. I am background,
atmosphere. I am freezing
my tits off. The kid who plays
peek-a-boo behind me
is called off by his mother towards
Iceland. Somewhere, in an office in the city,
a slightly greener version of me
flickers on a screen. Sometimes,
the wind runs a hand through my hair, but mostly
tired people sit on the bench in front of me
and smoke. I shade
no lovers. No birds will ever build
a nest in me. Nobody will ever call me home.

3

New Build

All this was factories but no one needs that
now. This place? This place is a breakthrough
in how to live we heard or maybe in
marketing. Here there are homes, attractive
boxes, complete with roofs and walls, these people
containers. We moved in here last July.

Doing their impressions of each other,
our houses stand round, silly as TV stars,
on Honeysuckle Drive and Summerberry
Avenue. Outside with Sunday hoses,
we pour water on our one means of
escape; at each door, hanging baskets are

lynched. Weekends, we stay in, as our houses
check themselves out in each other's windows.
Here live the young, the families: our smooth,
smooth roads are unvisited by police
or hearse. The pizza driver's engine purrs
through double glazing like a hearthside cat.

Debbie says, she thinks we'll never leave.
These summer nights, we're out in our back garden:
only the labels on our beer bottles
sweat. We throw ribs on the barbecue,
send laughter to the sky with the smoke.
Then we watch our children gnaw these bones.

Newport Talking

Me? I get up early, see. I like
to watch the sunrise over the Transporter,
to sneak, perhaps, one cheeky fag, to gently
blow the smoke away: as the fog clears,
the sun shines down on all these people. Really

bloody busy's what the next hour is,
changing all the traffic lights to go,
helping school kids safely cross the road,
and as for him who sits in his high ride
and winds the window down, and offers some
imaginative or foul-mouthed advice
to her in the next lane – well he can wait
and wait. Two hours of that, I like to stop

for lunch in the high fields which no one thinks
I have, take in the view, the air, and share
my butties with the horses, all those gorgeous
stinking bastards there, whose only speed
is slowness, their tails Sunday fishing line
dropped in the day, whose chewing is hypnosis.
An hour of them is everything I need
to set me up for my big afternoon

around the shops: my lovely sticky-up
paving stones put paid to this shoplifter,
a nudge, a wink, and this raincloud is shifted
from here above the head of this old lady
who's forgotten her umbrella. Rush
hour's a pain in my chest, the noise,
the stress, the traffic flow, the fuel emissions
up my nose. It's Friday night, and soon

my streets are dancefloors for these Brylcreem'd madmen,
these blowdry princesses, in all their giggling
height of fashion. How I love to see them –
how I tip the wink to skull-haired doormen,
line up taxis, fling the doors of chippies
wide, wide open, how I make the most
of every single moment, for I know
full well how this will end. It's 4am

and hours since I should have been in bed,
but who will watch if I don't? Here, outside
Debenhams, flat on his back, this bloke
with his big arms wrapped tight around the air.
I've seen him crossing, re-crossing my bridges,
staring too long down from there, to where
the bubbling reflection of the stars is.
Now I hover close to check his breath,
he shuffles in his sleep here in this doorway,
here in the place exactly where my heart is.

Valleys Village as a Tourist Attraction

Its splendours were found out by word of mouth,
the internet, when one celebrity
named it to another who misheard,
when *Lonely Planet* unexpectedly
placed it in its must-sees for the year,
having bodged it with some nook or hamlet
on the south coast, famous for its aspect
of the sea, a nosh-up joint, mentioned
by him off the TV. Within a week,

the lane from Mrs Moore's to Mitchem's dairy
was clogged with buses with onboard TVs,
tinted windows, air con, beverage holders,
a ride-on ducking stool or lavatory.
Folk walked the streets, medallion'd by cameras,
a neighbour's was turned into a boutique –
Authentic Artisan Crafts she had sourced
from Tesco – and, in kitchens, mams were working
like the clappers to meet all the needs
of their start-up living room-cum-bistros
fathers maître d'd. Some other parts

were worse. To look up at our tree'd or gorgeous
mountains was to see them dark and moving
with people, local women cooled on boyfriends,
husbands, strolled in heels which set the village
echoing. The way the next part started

isn't clear: maybe some rich stranger
said something about somebody's daughter
and someone's father overheard, or maybe
someone said that our iconic statue
of a cuckoo looked a little more
like a blackbird, but as was later claimed,
how can you tell who threw the first stone really
when so many hands are raised? So it was

something then, to look out the next morning
and see a bus's burnt-out skeleton,
the traveller's cheques confetti-ing the scene,
and resting up there, look, on the phone wires,
a line of passports with their open wings.

Among it all, our village's street sweeper,
alone there in the middle of the road,
like Gary Cooper stands there in *High Noon*,
was looking round, with lots of work to do.

One Fine Day

As usual that morning, I headed for the motorway,
got to the end of my street, found a roadblock there.
I shouted to the guard, 'What's going on?'
He had a shaving cut on his upper lip,
held his rifle in trembling hands.
'Government orders,' he said. 'I can't let you leave the street.'

I turned round, headed for the other end of the street,
where I found a sentry tower blocking my way.
This guard swigged from a hip flask, keeping one hand
on his holster. I heard a helicopter somewhere up there,
as he leaned in at my window, wiped his lips:
'Listen pal, you've got ten seconds. Skedaddle. Vamoose. Jog on.'

Back home, I phoned into work, turned Sky News on.
But when I told the kids we couldn't leave the street,
they yelled, 'No school!' They were practically doing backflips.
'Can we go and call for Scotty?' Even my wife said, 'A day
off work – thank God. Brenda's been such a bitch. Now listen, there's
something I need you to do.' She led me upstairs by the hand.

By lunchtime, everyone was lending a hand,
laying all the good stuff from their fridges on
patio tables they'd set up, lining the road. There
was bunting. We grabbed a bottle, headed out into the street
to join our neighbours, chatted the afternoon away,
our homemade trifle clinging to their lips.

Then Don, from next door, his lips
black with my shiraz, offered me his hand:
'Listen,' he said, 'all that last summer with your right of way –
I don't know what I was thinking.' I said, 'Don,
forget it. You're a bloke. You're just a legend in this street.
Now listen, have you got any more of that homebrew there?'

With that, Mick and Dave from no. 8 cranked up their
PA, sent a message to our hips,
and in seconds we were all up and dancing in the street.
Even the nervous guard put his gun down, took the hand
of Frank Miller's daughter, and they got their boogie on.

The mother of all headaches next day. On my way
to the car, I saw Don get in his van, shouted 'Alright there?,'
but he had his hands-free in. Then he sped off for the motorway,
clipping the kerb, blowing exhaust fumes all over our street.

Postman

The man who knows exactly where you live
plunges his hand in the lucky dip

he carries on his shoulder, conjures up
your day: the papers, packages, the words

to make you sing this morning or to stop
your heart. *Sign here*, he grins, with something from

the court, or offers you a bill and whistles
badly. Early hours he puts the creak

of your garden gate into a horror movie,
leaves his footprints all over your drive,

with his clean conscience and his paid-for stride.
His day starts any time before the day does;

he goes to bed as early as a child
and sleeps so well – as well as you would like

to face a day of carrying that sack –
the weight of all those futures, on your back.

The Landlord at The Philanthropic

From here behind the bar he drives the world,
or pulls each pint as if he's shifting gear,
that huge mirror peering over his shoulder
or stabbing him in the back,
by showing the world what he's got up his sleeve
or the small truth
of his bald patch. He has by heart the melody
of coins dropping into the jukebox, is at an age between old
and young, has a perfect memory for the birthdays
of regulars, a dance step, a backslap, the chit-chat
for everyone. Now he sends a half-pint glass
twirling, spinning, whirling through the world
and picks it from the air, now looks
out of the corner of his eye
to spot some trouble, somewhere over there,
him with his firm grip on glasses, change, the shoulder
of him who's gone too far or had too much.
One glance can take you in
and weigh you up, tell the dangerous bloke
from the servable drunk. Now
he asks this battered-looking boy
again if he'd like to double up
on that vodka shot, now he winks and drops
his voice to a whisper, and this bubbling girl
leans and leans across the bar to hear. At twelve,
at one, he bolts the door firmly against
all his friends, checks the till
and pours himself one drink – *one* drink –
of milk. Soon he'll be sleeping soundly in the room
above his life, but now he looks round
at this echoing place, at these dreg-filled lies,
this after-party that's empty and all his,
at the man there growing older in the mirror,
raising and raising a glass to his own lips.

Mad Pete

You'd see him at all hours, pedalling through
the city, making cycle lanes of every
pavement or else on the motorway,
drawing v-signs from the cabs of lorries,
with his wobbly amble or his darting

stumble. What he wore was a worksite
fluoro-vest, t-shirt, ripped jeans, and carried
on his back the thing which made him mad:
a massive sandwich board, scrawled with handwriting –
When will we stop the capitalist cabal

+ *their Freemasons?* He made us wonder, question:
all the talk was he was kindly, harmless,
had been seen walking calmly through the city,
pointing tourists in the right direction,
and one night Big Jim picked him up from where he'd

fallen victim to a puncture, gave him
a lift home, and he left him with a handshake,
a crumpled fiver to cover the petrol.
Nonetheless, he was unmoved, insistent:
a day, the bike, the sandwich board. Then things

got worse, got different: for three days running,
at rush hour, his bike on the hard shoulder,
while he just sat there on the roundabout
with coffee and his thumb out, causing a
distraction. That was one thing. But another

was the night he was spotted on the wrong side
of the barrier, on the overpass,
holding on tight, as the sandwich board
fluttered in the wind like washing, traffic
wooshing past beneath him. Every life

is someone's own. When I think of him now,
I think of him one night outside The Dog:
my taxi fare gone on a final round,
I saw him pass, asked for a backy home.
He turned, and paused, and offered a shy wave.

He said he was already carrying too much weight.

The Red Lady of Paviland

Scientists open the curtains, wake her with light,
and there she is, who's only bits of bone.
There she is look, up there in that cave,
preserved by history, by sheets of ice

and accident. The jigsaw puzzle of her:
the firewood of the tibia and fibula, the washed-up
ship's hull of the ribcage, the pianist's
fingers of the toes. Scientists open the curtains,

wake her with light, and there she lies, advertising
what it is we come to. They slander her
with theories: that she was murdered
by smugglers, the sex toy

of Roman soldiers. Scientists open the curtains,
wake her with light, and she waits for history
to catch up with her, for science
to tell us what she really is:

male, twenty-five to thirty years old
at death, unusually robust for his age, partial
to seafood. He knew an earth
where mammoths, where sabre-toothed tigers

strolled, and now there he lies, the autojumble
of him, his bits and parts. When they roll away the stone,
when scientists open the curtains, wake him with light,
he'd whisper, if he could, the thing he is:

the first Welshman. The place where all this starts.

Cofiwch Dryweryn

Tryweryn

It is so still. The water
presses its mute button. Here, you can look
in any direction and just see hills
and, in the lake, the hills' reflection.
Breaking the surface, the tip of the spire
of the waterlogged church
is a radio aerial bringing the news
of another century to those submerged.

If you could step now into the water
and swim down, down, find the wreck
of a town, spend an hour doggy-paddling
down a main street cat's-eyed by starfish,
watch fish blowing bubbles in a shop window
and, in a school you well remember,
take a book from the shelf,
brush a shell from the cover... Then jemmy open

the rusted door of the postbox, take a letter
with a lover's name on the cover, snatch a suitcase
from the hand of a girl with seaweed in her hair,
waiting for a bus on the corner
that'll never be there... Could you give the past
a piggyback to the surface, then stand on the bank
and open the letter to find those pages
blank, blank, and don't have the heart

to open the book, pick the lock on the suitcase?
Sunset does Morse code on the lake surface.
Wind shakes the hill like a picnic blanket.
In the city, a polished historian
picks up a pen. In Liverpool,
a man turns the tap, fills the sink or a glass
and, in Tryweryn, the lowering water
makes the church spire grow stronger, taller.

Last Day of School, Capel Celyn, 1963

Two rows of them, two rows of smiling kids.
Two at the back alike enough for twins
in shirts and ties, like Mam dressed them for this,
looks on their faces like the teacher, forceful-
bosomed there behind them just said *Listen,*
you better sit there and behave and said it
in the voice she says that in. A little
girl there in the front row does a vacant
look which seems to say *I'm at that stage*
of youngness, me, I really don't know where
the hell I am, while the boy next to her
is squinting like a sniper and his target's
the dude who made him sit still with these shoes on.
Two rows of children on a sunny day.
Two rows of kids who've fretted months away
since they were told the news, can't stop believing –
however many times the teacher tells them –
that when the water comes it will come quickly
and wash the world, and wash the world away.

The Remains

The families who had relatives buried at Capel Celyn were given the option to leave the remains where they were or to have them moved to the new memorial garden.
      – Einion Thomas, *Capel Celyn: Ten Years of Destruction*

Four men in shirtsleeves on a summer's day.
You wonder how much they were being paid.
Four men out sweating on a summer's day
with shovels and grimaces, with mouths
to feed. Four men standing up to breathe
or wipe a brow, then falling to again.
Four fathers or four hard-working men.

The cemetery is calm today, the chapel
half-demolished now. Four men toss earth
over their shoulders till, a few feet down,
they hit the coffin. Then, with care and rope,
they bear the weight of death up to the top.
The first of eight, for the families who've
chosen to have their loved ones moved.

And when the work is done, they'll drive them out
to this memorial built on the banks
of the lake this will be: neat rows of newly
polished headstones, good views, the largely
untroubled earth. It's just the sort of place
to make you think *Oh what a lovely place.*
What will they think, the dead, on their drive here?

And when the work is done, the cemetery
is buried under gravel, concrete: no
tapped message could ever make it through.
What would *you* do? A father turns away,
ruffles his daughter's head. His only son.
The way he always had to call and call him.
How he could never get him out of bed.

Aberfan

So here they come from the assembly hall.
So here they come, from where they have been singing
All Things Bright and Beautiful. So here
they come, this spring-limbed, bobtail bunch, these yay-high

heroes, ragamuffins, making slipstreams
of their ties, who kick the air with joy
at being them, who rush from the headteacher's
voice chasing them down the corridor,

this one walking quickly with her head down
and saying her times table in her head,
this one tapping this one on the shoulder
to whisper something – there! – about her brother,

this one (he's a monkey) taking bets
on what he might or might not do at breaktime.
So here they come around the corner now,
with their baddie'd knees, their untied laces,

their tendency to spend the morning gazing
somewhere over there, into the classroom.
They settle in their chairs. The world breathes in.
And now pause there. And now, oh now, pause there.

4

Girl

So look she has those eyes the sort of eyes
of any girl look who has eyes that colour,

and if her walk is made for whoops or sighs,
it moves her look from one place to another,

and when she sings or whistles birds don't gather
and open up their beaks to harmonise,

and if she giggles look or if she cries,
the world spins on, about the same as ever,

and if her cheekbones draw their share of *My-
oh-mys*, she only stole them from her mother,

and there's nothing in her to lionise,
to drive me look to sonnets or to murder,

or words to tell you what she's really like.
Or words to say how much that bloody matters.

On Hearing You Have Lost Your New Love

So right now girl I guess you find it hard
to eat, and as for sleep that's something you
remember doing once, and memories
you have are just your memories of him,
his face is in the kettle, in the fridge,
the ceiling right above your bed, beneath
your lovely eyelids every time you dare
to close them – there – and any second now
he'll show up at the door you know, you know,
and bottles line up on the coffee table
like trophies for surviving one more hour,
you check your phone again and make a wish.
I guess with you that's roughly how it is.
There is a reason girl I know all this.

Couple Kissing Against the Wall of a Pub

They're kissing here, all through the afternoon.
They're kissing, giving all the cars a view
of love, as they're stopped at the traffic lights,
and everyone's pretending not to stare.
They're kissing and they're coming up for air,
to smile and laugh and pinch, to look into
each other's eyes again. Beneath the glare
of neon, here, on this gum-spattered street,
this boy, this girl: their hands so tight, *so* tight,
round necks, round waists, or in each other's hair.
A man at the pub door tots up his change,
a woman lugs her week home underarm
in Tesco bags which cut into her hands
and here, beneath the sign of The Old Mill,
they're smooching still. They shuffle and they switch,
now him, now her, back to the wall, the bricks,
and looking out at all of this. They're what,
nineteen? In tracky bottoms, skinny jeans,
they wrap themselves around each other, wear
each other's limbs like clothes, and now they reach
a hand, a finger, to a face, a cheek,
in disbelief. Me? *Me?* A gull swoops down
to peck at a kebab, and now they shift
again, and she's a copper, searching him.
What will she find? A billboard, overhead,
is advertising someone else's life,
phone wires carry fragments of despair,
and these two, here, against a wall, they tickle,
chuckle, whisper in each other's ears.
Is it too much to say the traffic's stopped
because of them? Who wouldn't look, or want
a love this fierce? Now, at the green light,
these quiet, gleaming, air-conditioned cars
pull off, a little quicker than they might.

When I'm Gone,

don't do this, babe: as they lower my bones
to the ground, the grave, please don't leap down
to be with me, don't take the good, fresh earth

and wipe it on your face or underneath
your skirt to be with me, don't take your lunch,
your dinner, at the cemetery, to eat

with me, or let them find you, huddling
at dawn by my grave, shivering, cuddling
my headstone. Don't. Don't wear my scent, my clothes

to be with me, don't weep or wail or moan,
or turn to drink or God and don't give up
on job or joy or life to be with me,

to be with me. Don't do that, babe. And don't
give me cause to hear that other voice,
which whispers in my ear each time we're out,

and you look past me at some other bloke,
who grins, or turns to you, or meets your eye:
Fool, what if she don't need your advice?

The Girl in the Coffee Shop

is a girl and where she is is yes, you know,
a coffee shop. *Be more precise.* She's there

at the next table, I could just up now
and talk to her. What is she like? Extremely

like herself. And what's she doing? Smoking
(the café is outside, there's – *woosh!* – the breeze)

and I confess that I would cough and hate it
if I were sitting next to her. I am:

I will. She looks round at a coughing bloke
and chases smoke with a sip of some brightly

orange liquid. There she sits, smokes, drinks,
out on the street here in the afternoon,

our nicotine-addicted, possibly
mildly alcoholic girl, with all

the things she has, with all that massive, gorgeous
Fuck you to time she's doing. Now the clock

is ticking in the square. The waiter tries
and tries to read this over my plaid shoulder

and me, I sip and think of all my problems.
She clicks her fingers and she yells out *Garçon!*

★

Meanwhile, the bloke who's walking down the street
is in the street and walking. He has thoughts

he has, plus this: a cracking jacket. He
has hair that does this: grows out of his head,

or moves now in the air like any drugged
Russian gymnast. Meanwhile, our girl

is high on life and looking out from here
to where he'll pass who's nicely-jacketed

and just her type. The bloke? He's nothing much,
his jacket is the sort you'd see and spend

a lifetime searching for in every backstreet
shop. His walk? It's good, it's good, well hell,

you could just look at him and say he walks
expertly. A bloke with all his thoughts,

that kind of youth like *What's the world but this
that I could walk across?* The clock is ticking

in the square and me, I sit and sip
and there, the polish-shoed or huffish waiter

brings our girl's second drink so slowly over,
it's like he's saying *Garçon? Really? Garçon?!*

★

Meanwhile, the girl there in the coffee shop
lights up another cigarette of course

and coughs of course. Imagine if the cloud
of smoke she's blowing out grew now to fill

this café, square, this world, and what life was
was feeling through the smoke to where she was

fumblingly... She holds a cigarette
in that hand and her orange drink in this,

like on the sunny afternoon this is,
what counts is keeping things in balance, things

in equilibrium. The waiter's way
of jangling all the change he has in his

bumbag, that's annoying really, when
I'm trying to do this. A horse huffs past,

soundtracked by clip-clopping coconut halves
its hooves do, carriage filled with tourists who

make all of this a photo. That clock *is*
there in the square and on the table there,

our girl, her fingernails are drumming, drumming,
like what she's doing's waiting there for something.

★

Meanwhile, the bloke who's walking down the street
is doing that, is running his right hand

through his nice hair. He thinks of being him:
the weather's fine, the day is one with no

complications, and his jacket is
spectacular. *Nice horse* he thinks, as he

comes round the corner with his father's walk
and his own shoes and all the horse's thoughts

are lost to history. Our girl? Still here
and looking out at where he'll pass, as now

it moves, the afternoon, towards its big
dramatic bit. She springs up now to greet him,

this boy she knows, is meeting, and she holds
him close, our tipsy girl, one moment, two,

and makes his jacket into something to
inhale. They break and look and what smiles are

are theirs and bloody huge and in the square
that clock is ticking and, right now, I sit

and sip a bit, wave to the waiter, for
another coffee while I'm writing this.

★

So there they go, our couple, hand-in-hand,
one gorgeous-jacketed and one a little

wobbly on her feet, puffing a cloud
that might just turn to rain if it could rain

on me here, now, and make the thing complete.
The way they walk's in the direction of

the evening, and as they make their way
through crowds which bob and lurch, which thicken, thin,

those hands now stretch, now shift, but do not slip,
till all they are's a little plume of smoke

away there at the far end of the street,
that you could make your future if you ran

from here to there. Meanwhile, we're watching them,
me and the waiter, sipping, serving, waiting,

watching men. He slides the coin she's left
into his jangling belt then, all at once,

he sits down in her chair, as if to see
the way things look from there. He stretches out

his legs, he takes her glass, that inch of drink,
and sighing, grinning, raises it to me.

The Bicycle

I was driving home when I first saw it,
in the mirror there behind me,
put my foot down and forgot it.
Coming to a few miles later
at traffic lights, I blinked to spot it
pulling up again behind me.
That fluoro-strip, that dynamo –
how had it managed to stay with me?

I decided on the long way home,
the hilly way, the car at sixty
through all those corners. Twenty minutes
and I was dawdling at a T-junction
when look, that bicycle again:
I saw the rider was a woman,
blonde, mid-twenties, there, a face
I thought I knew but couldn't place.

Ready to give up now, curious,
I ambled the last half-mile home,
keeping her there in the rear-view mirror,
but when I turned the tight last corner,
I looked and saw she'd disappeared.
I pulled into a lay-by, waited
for moments there of muffled panic,
before I turned back to look for her.

If home is the end of every journey,
maybe I'll get back there someday.
Until then you might spot me, reader,
scouring these roads, these hedges,
hollow-eyed behind this wheel,
looking for a flash of light,
a face I think I recognise,
an upturned bicycle, a scrap of dream.

Song

So come to me, by plane, by train, by car,
by unicycle, girl, by self-drive van,
by Twitter, FaceTime or by sleight-of-hand,
oh lease yourself a pack-mule, a giraffe,
oh steal yourself a moped, pay a man
to carry you here, girl, on piggyback,
or get the railway to lay extra track
up to my door, up to my waiting hands.

So come to me, on fresh air or on credit,
oh hoof it, leg it, go by Shanks's pony
over stony ground and live off grass
or hedgerow, girl, whatever you can forage,
and rest on river banks, beneath a roof
of forest. Navigate your way by stars
or GPS, but listen, girl, be quick.
Oh speed yourself towards my waiting skin.

So come to me. Oh score yourself a gun,
a false moustache, girl, and a native tongue,
and smuggle yourself in the early hours
under wire and across the border.
Or buy yourself a wrecked and promising
motorhome and let dawn find you, girl,
with oil-stained cheeks, just working till it purrs
or goes. Oh drive towards my waiting bones.

So come, by raft, by hovercraft, or do
a goose-fat, nose-clipped, brave or water-winged
breaststroke through the sea that's parting me
from you, or fit a tractor engine to
a li-lo, rubber ring, a rowing boat.
My home's made by these hands, this skin, these bones.
My home is made of straw and fragile stars.
Oh come to me. Oh make this where you are.

Notes

'The Red Lady of Paviland': the poem's title is the name given to a skeleton, discovered at the Goat's Hole Cave at Paviland, on the Gower Peninsula, in 1823 by William Buckland, professor of geology at Oxford University. Assuming the skeleton to be female, Buckland established a number of theories as to who she was and the life she had lived. Science has since shown that the skeleton is that of a young man, who lived 29,000 years ago, the oldest modern human skeleton found in Britain.

'Cofiwch Dryweryn': this sequence focuses on the history of the Tryweryn valley and the village of Capel Celyn in North Wales, which was forcibly evacuated and turned into a reservoir in the 1960s, in order to provide a water source for Liverpool. It draws partly on an interview the author conducted with David Walters, who was arrested for his part in an attack on the electricity transformer at the dam site in 1962. The sequence's title comes from graffiti painted on a wall near Llanrhystud, Ceredigion in the early 1960s by the poet Meic Stephens, and translates as 'Remember Tryweryn.'

Acknowledgements

Some of these poems have appeared in *Hwaet!* (Bloodaxe), *The Tree Line* (Worple) and *The Wenlock Poetry Festival Anthology 2015 & 2016* (Fair Acre); and in *Barrow Street*, *The Frogmore Papers*, *The High Window*, *The Interpreter's House*, *New Welsh Reader*, *The North*, *Orbis*, *Planet*, *Poetry News*, *Poetry Review*, *Poetry Wales*, *The Reader*, *Red Poets*, *Southword* and *Wales Arts Review*.

'Servant Minding a Seat for his Master Before a Performance of *The Rivals*, Covent Garden Theatre, 1775' received first prize in the Ledbury Festival Poetry Competition 2014. 'Kurt Cobain Proposes to Courtney Love, TJs, Newport, December 1991' received first prize in the Oxford Brookes Poetry Competition 2017. 'On Hearing You Have Lost Your New Love' received second prize in the Guernsey International Poetry Competition 2018. 'Newport Talking' was commissioned by Swansea University as part of the fiftieth anniversary commemorations of the death of Vernon Watkins. Many thanks to Owen Sheers.

The author wishes to acknowledge the support of a Literature Wales Published Writer's Bursary to work on this collection in 2016, and an Arthur Welton Award from the Society of Authors in 2017.

For their help and advice with this collection, I am extremely grateful to Saskia Barnden, Rhian Edwards, John Freeman, Matthew Jarvis, Nadia Kingsley, David Morley, Matt Nunn, Benjamin Palmer and Amy Wack. For help with the Tryweryn poems, thanks to Petra Bennett, Dylan Iorwerth and David Walters. Enormous thanks to all friends and supporters of *My Family and Other Superheroes*. Thank you beyond measure to my parents.